by Charlene Gieck

BALD EAGLES

Bald Eagle Magic for Kids

Gareth Stevens Children's Books
MILWAUKEE

For a free color catalog describing Gareth Stevens' list of high-quality children's books, call 1-800-341-3569 (USA) or 1-800-461-9120 (Canada).

Library of Congress Cataloging-in-Publication Data

Gieck, Charlene
    Bald eagle magic for kids / by Charlene Gieck; photographs by Tom and Pat Leeson, and Bob Baldwin.
        p. cm. -- (Animal magic for kids)
    Includes index.
    Summary: Examines the habitat, physical characteristics, behavior, abuse, and protection of the bald eagle.
    ISBN 0-8368-0761-8
    1. Bald eagle--Juvenile literature. [1. Bald eagle. 2. Eagles.]
    I. Leeson, Tom, ill. II. Leeson, Pat, Ill. III. Baldwin, Bob. 1948- ill. IV. Title. V. Series.
    QL696.F32G53   1991
    598'.916-dc20   91-50552

This North American edition published by
Gareth Stevens Children's Books
1555 North RiverCenter Drive, Suite 201
Milwaukee, Wisconsin 53212, USA

First published in 1991 by NorthWord Press, Inc., with text copyright © 1991 by Charlene Gieck and photographs copyright © by Tom Leeson, Pat Leeson, and Bob Baldwin. Copyright © 1991 by NorthWord Press, Inc.

Printed in MEXICO.

1 2 3 4 5 6 7 8 9 97 96 95 94 93 92

But you never were made, as I,
On the wings of the wind to fly!
The eagle said.

— Will Carleton

Getting to Know Eagles

We all know the bald eagle. It's the national symbol of the United States. When we think of the eagle, we usually think of things like strength, dignity and freedom. In 1782, these qualities inspired the leaders of the United States to place the bald eagle on the country's Great Seal. Since then, the bald eagle has been a common feature on posters, business signs and even U.S. currency.

For centuries, native Americans have admired the bald eagle. The eagle was often carved at the very top of their totem poles, the place of highest respect. Because eagles are able to soar high into the sky and disappear from sight, the Pueblo people believed the eagle was related to the Sun. They prized eagle feathers, believing the feathers would carry their prayers to the heavens. Eagle feathers are used yet today in tribal religious rites or awarded to persons performing deeds of great valor.

The eagle is honored by native Americans in the eagle dance which is still performed at many powwows today.

The dignified image of the bald eagle comes partly from its coloration - a pure white head and tail contrasted with a dark brown body. It's almost as if it is dressed for a formal event. This coloration makes the bald eagle easy to see, even from a distance. Adult bald eagles are easy to identify.

Eagles don't get those white feathers right away. During the first four to five years of life, an eagle's feathers are dark brown, including those on the head and tail. These brown eagles are called "immatures." Immatures often have white

feathers under their wings and on their chests. The amount of white varies with each eagle. Young immature eagles are often confused with golden eagles and hawks. By five years of age, all bald eagles have the white head and tail. They are now ready to breed and have their own families.

If the bald eagle has feathers on its head, then why is it called bald? The name comes from an Old English word, "balde," which means "white." So it was natural to call this pure white-headed bird the bald eagle.

Their large size and the fierce look in their eyes give eagles the appearance of strength. The bald eagle has a wingspan of seven to eight feet. Try spreading your arms to your sides and have someone measure your "wingspan." Are you bigger than an eagle?

Female eagles are about forty inches tall. They are larger than male eagles which measure about thirty inches tall. Even though eagles appear to be huge, they are not very heavy. They only weigh eight to fourteen pounds. Their large appearance comes from many layers of feathers. Like most other birds, they have hollow bones to make them lightweight for flying. Struts or braces inside the hollow bones keep the bones from breaking easily.

A seven-foot wingspan can make it difficult to get into the air. Once in flight, though, the long broad wings are ideal for hours of soaring over the countryside. Eagles use moving air currents to make travel effortless and quick. During a good journey, they will seldom flap their wings.

Eagles are "birds of prey," which means they eat meat. Fish is the favorite food of eagles. Eagles are not fussy eaters and will eat most types of fish, caught alive or found dead. They eat many animals besides fish, including geese, ducks, rabbits, turtles and other small animals. They also eat *carrion* – the decaying flesh of dead animals, such as a deer hit by a car. Carrion is especially important in winter, when other foods are not easily found.

To catch fish, eagles generally watch the water surface from a perch or while soaring in the air. Then they swoop down close to the water and drop their feet right in the water to catch the fish. Many times they miss their target and have to try again and again.

Eagles often steal food from other eagles or from other birds of prey, such as ospreys. Eagles are opportunistic feeders, eating almost anything that is available.

You might be called "eagle-eyed" if you have good vision and notice things quickly. Eagles have excellent eyesight. They can see six to eight times better than you. An eagle can see a rabbit two miles away! You would need a good pair of binoculars to see that well. Good eyesight is very important to an eagle soaring high over a lake, looking for lunch.

The *talons*, or claws, on an eagle's toes are curved and razor-sharp for catching and holding its prey. This gives eagles the name *raptor*, which comes from a Latin word "rapere," meaning to grip or grasp. Rough bumps on the eagle's toes also help it hold slippery, wiggling fish. The raptor uses its feet to protect itself. With its long talons and vise like grip, it can inflict serious wounds to intruders.

An Eagle's Life

Male and female eagles usually spend most of the winter apart. When they find each other again in late winter, they perform courtship displays including "cartwheels" in mid-air. The display starts when one bird flips on its back in the air and grasps the talons of the other bird.

Together they spiral down through the air like a cartwheel. Just when you think they will crash into the ground, they separate. Then they fly back up into the air to continue courtship. This activity is thought to bond the birds to each other.

Nest building begins shortly after courtship. Gathering sticks for the nest takes a long time, and both birds help. The nest, or *aerie*, is a large stick structure. When it's first built, a nest may measure three feet wide by three feet deep. Pine branches or grasses line the nest, making a soft layer for the young eagles.

If the pair nested together before, they will probably use their old nest again. Since more sticks will be added, nests get larger and larger each year. The largest nest ever found was in Ohio. It was nearly nine feet wide and twelve feet deep. It was probably bigger than your bedroom. Most nests are as big as your bed.

The area around the pair's nest is called a *territory*. It is fiercely defended from intruders. Other eagles and birds are driven out of the area by the pair of nesting eagles.

Eagles need several things for nesting: a large tree, a source of food and peace and quiet. They usually nest near rivers or lakes so they can be close to sources of fish. The nest tree will usually be a living pine tree, but aspen, oak, cotton-wood and other trees are used too. The tree they choose will always be the one that towers above other trees around it. Since eagles like to be able to see what's around them, the nest is built near the top of the tree.

One to three eggs are laid in early spring. Eagle eggs are plain white and close in size to a goose egg. The female sits on, or incubates, the eggs for 35-40 days. The male shares in incubating the eggs or brings food to his mate. He can often be seen perching close by, keeping a watchful eye for trouble.

When the eggs hatch, the emerging tiny eaglets are covered with thick brown down. These special fluffy feathers keep the eaglets warm until their regular feathers develop. The eaglets are helpless, unable to walk or stand up. It's hard to believe that these unusual-looking little creatures will someday look like their regal parents.

The adults are now kept very busy finding food for these always hungry babies. The female eagle carefully tears the meat into small pieces and puts it into the eaglets' mouths. Eaglets grow quickly and are soon able to move around in the nest and start grabbing at food as soon as it arrives.

When they are about three weeks old, the chicks start growing dark brown feathers. Most of the eaglets' time is spent eating, sleeping, caring for their feathers and exercising their tiny wings. By three months of age, the eaglets are ready for *fledging* or taking their first flight. Sometimes the first flight is by accident. Either a sibling knocks them out of the nest or the wind catches them when they're on the edge of the nest.

If they are lucky, they will flutter to a nearby perch and later fly back to the nest. If they are unlucky, they can end up on the ground. The adults may not care for them if they cannot see them in the grass and brush under the tree. Some will die because they cannot return to the nest on their own.

Young eagles stay with the adults for approximately eight weeks after they learn to fly. The young soon learn to hunt for their own food.

As late fall approaches, young eagles start moving southward. They have now learned how to hunt and to take care of themselves. These eagles, now called immatures, leave the nest area before the adults.

Records show that some nest sites have been used for more than thirty years. Eagles that survive the difficult first years of life can live to be up to forty years old. Some eagles kept in captivity have lived to be as much as fifty years old.

Where Eagles Live

Bald eagles are found only in North America. At one time, they nested along rivers and lakes throughout Canada and the United States, except Hawaii, where they have never nested. Hundreds of eagles can still be found in the states of Minnesota, Wisconsin, Michigan, Washington, Oregon and Florida. Thousands of eagles are located in Alaska and throughout Canada.

Nesting sites are near forested lakes and rivers in areas with little disturbance. Eagles are cautious of humans. The sight of an approaching person can cause the adult birds to leave the nest. When this happens, the eggs or young may become chilled and die. If you are hiking or boating, stay away from eagle nests. Watch them only from a distance. Use binoculars instead of trying to get too close.

Eagle *migration* occurs each spring and fall. Adults will also travel south in the winter if the northern rivers and lakes freeze over. Large groups of eagles can be found near dams on major rivers where the moving water does not freeze. The Mississippi River is a very important waterway for bald eagles. Wildlife refuges in many areas offer protection for wintering eagles.

Winter is a great time to watch eagles. You can watch them from your car, which acts as a blind that keeps you hidden from the eagle's sight. Watching from your car also lets you enjoy this activity from a warm spot. Many states along the Mississipi River now hold special eagle-watching events. Many people are learning a lot about eagles.

In the United States, the National Wildlife Federation counts the number of eagles each winter. In 1990, the total number of eagles seen was 13,574. That's a lot of eagles! This number doesn't include the thousands of eagles in Alaska, but it does include the eagles that live in Canada during the summer months.

Types of Eagles

Approximately sixty species of eagles occur in the world. There are four types of eagles – sea eagles, booted eagles, buteonine eagles and serpent eagles.

Sea Eagles: The bald eagle is part of this group. Sea eagles are found nearly worldwide along wooded seacoasts, lakes and rivers. They are not present in South America. They have combinations of dark and white feathers. They have short, bare legs and toes with long, sharp talons. They feed primarily on fish, but will eat waterfowl, mammals, turtles and carrion. Sea eagles have long, broad wings and short, wedge-shaped tails. Their large nests are made of sticks and built in tall trees.

Booted Eagles: The golden eagle belongs in this group. Booted eagles live on wooded and barren mountains throughout Europe and Asia and in northern Africa and western North America. Most are dark brown in color; the golden eagle has golden feathers on its head and on the back of its neck. Booted eagles feed on rabbits, rodents, snakes, birds and carrion. They are called " booted" because they have feathers down to their toes. Their nests are usually found on the ledges of rocky cliff faces.

Buteonine Eagles: These, including the harpy eagle, are the largest and most powerful of eagles. They live in dense, tropical jungles of Mexico, the Philippines and South America. Buteonine eagles have crested heads, giving them a witchlike appearance. Their short, broad wings make them able to move around in thick jungles. Their diet consists of birds and tree-dwelling mammals, such as monkeys. Their nests are built in trees.

Serpent Eagles: The bateleur eagle is a well known representative of this group. Serpent eagles are found in the tropical grasslands of Africa, Europe, Asia and Australia. They have short tails in comparison with other eagles. Their short, bare legs are covered with rough scales. Their toes are strong and short. They eat snakes, insects, fish, mammals and birds. Tall, broad-topped trees are where their nests are found.

It's Hard Being An Eagle

The bald eagle is classified as an endangered species. This means that at one time, we feared that this great bird would disappear forever. The number of eagles dropped quickly in the early 1950s and 60s. DDT, a powerful and long-lasting poison used to protect crops from insects, was used widely after World War II. Unfortunately, DDT killed more than pests. Fish and birds began dying after eating insects treated with DDT. Eagles were affected when they ate the dead fish or birds.

DDT caused eagles to lay thin-shelled eggs. The eggs broke under the weight of female eagles as they tried to incubate the eggs. The number of eagles declined when no young were produced for many years. The United States banned DDT in 1972, and eagle populations have been growing slowly ever since. But eagles have other problems. They encounter hunters and disease, and they may collide with utility poles or vehicles. Also, many of the tall trees that eagles use as nest trees have been cut down for lumber. Lakeshores have too often become places for homes and businesses. And many lakes have become too busy with people boating and fishing. Eagles need solitude.

We know a great deal about eagles now. In many places, nest locations are put on maps and checked each year. Young eagles are often banded with small aluminum leg bands. The band has a unique number that identifies the eagle for life. When the eagle is handled at a later time, the band tells researchers how old the eagle is and where it hatched.

The Bald Eagle Protection Act, a U.S. federal law, was created to protect eagles. It prevents eagle nest trees from being cut down or disturbed. It also makes it illegal for people to possess any part of an eagle, even feathers. Large fines and jail sentences are designed to discourage people from harming the eagle. By protecting eagles, we are protecting a beautiful and important bird.

GLOSSARY

The words below also appear in the text in *italicized* type. The page number on which each word first appears is listed after each definition.

Aerie: The nest of a bird on a cliff or a mountaintop (page 19).

Carrion: Dead and decaying animal flesh (page 13).

Fledging: When a young bird is ready for flight (page 33).

Migration: A seasonal movement from one region to another (page 39).

Raptor: A bird with talons that are used for seizing prey (page 17).

Talons: The sharp claws of a bird of prey (page 17).

Territory: The area defended by an animal against others (page 21).

ADULT-CHILD INTERACTION QUESTIONS

These are questions you may ask young readers to get them to think about bald eagles as viable occupants of a niche in the food chain. Encourage them to explain their feelings about bald eagles and to ask their own questions. Clarify any misunderstandings they may have about the predator-prey relationship as it relates to bald eagles, and explain the need to have both predators and prey in the world. In this way, you can help foster future generations of environmentally aware and appreciative adults.

1. If you were a bald eagle, where would you build your nest?
    What would you feed to your young?

2. Does a bald eagle inspire certain feelings in you? What are they?

3. Why do some eagles move away from the nest sites in winter?

4. What are the differences between bald eagles and other eagles?

5. What are the differences between immature eagles and adult bald eagles?

6. Name some characteristics of birds of prey.